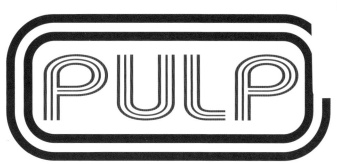

the
TOMORROW
PEOPLE

by
Susan Wilson

PHOTOGRAPHIC CREDITS

FRONT COVER: © Deluze © ALL ACTION

BACK COVER: Steve Double & C. Rikken © RETNA

© ALL ACTION

© LONDON FEATURES INTERNATIONAL

© REDFERNS

© RETNA

© REX FEATURES

First published in Great Britain 1996
UFO Music Ltd 18 Hanway Street
London W1P 9DD

The author and publishers have made every effort to contact all copyright holders. Any who for any reason have not been contacted are invited to write to the publishers so that a full acknowledgment may be made in subsequent editions of this work.

ISBN 1-873884-51-6

Designed by UFO Music Ltd

Printed and bound in Great Britain by
Butler & Tanner Ltd, Frome and London

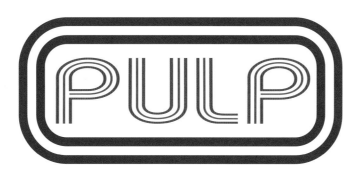

the TOMORROW PEOPLE

THE story you are about to read is an extraordinary one. It involves determination, courage, madness, poor judgement, bad timing, second hand clothes, masses of celebrities, sexual inadequacy, sexual triumph, close shaves with death, loss, gain, glory, and above all, self-belief. It veers between comedy and despair like an out of control car bouncing from one lamp post to another. But ultimately it reaches its destination like a battered pigeon coming home to roost. It is a remarkable, and truly inspiring story. Anyone who's ever nailed themselves to their dreams till they've bled all they can will recognise themselves in its pages. Especially if they've dragged them kicking and screaming into reality with a wry smile and an eye for detail. It's almost a fairy story. But try telling that to Jarvis. ●

COMMON PEOPLE

- PULP'S BRITAIN

"How can you get into Route 66 when you live off the M1?"

Last year, a rather poignant reminder of days gone by graced our television screens. It was only an advertisement for Capital Gold, one of London's cheesier radio stations, but it depicted a memorable era magnificently. Riding a bright orange Space Hopper, her hair stuck out in pigtail bunches, a little girl bounced into a grim front yard on a cold grey morning, just in time to catch the milkman snogging the neighbour. Naturally enough, the neighbour was resplendent in a knee length, powder blue negligee, her hair a delightfully artificial shade of blonde. A perfect snapshot of the Seventies, it could easily have been a scene from one of Pulp's videos.

The Seventies have long been celebrated by both pop and rock bands. Grunge, the compliant rock of the late Eighties and early Nineties was built on a wave of Black Sabbath, Led Zeppelin, second hand corduroys and skinny rib jumpers, but being an American phenomenon, it took its aesthetic cue more from The Brady Bunch than the Fenn Street Gang.

Britpop on the other hand (because loathsome though it might seem to the bands involved, such categorisation provides nice little reference points for journalists and fans alike) is exactly what it proclaims itself to be - pop with a distinctly British flavour. And its interpretation of the Seventies - which figure just as prominently style wise as they did in grunge - is peppered with echoes of vintage sit-coms and kid's programmes like Man About The House, On The Buses, Magpie and Please Sir. Britpop bands who don't favour contemporary Italian designer kagoules, swank about in collared anoraks, Adidas tracksuit tops, tank tops, Wrangler jeans, lurex polo necks and fat silk ties. Wide lapels and ill fitting trousers characterise the suits worn on the scene, and mini skirts and go-go boots decorate stages and dance floors. All is downbeat but colourful, and in the case of Pulp - who, you might be forgiven for thinking, have been doing this kind of thing since the Seventies started - everything glitters like gold. Or should that be gilt.

Pulp have formulated their very own tradition from the tawdry secrecy of suburbia, the small excitements tucked away inside the routine of everyday life, the chance meetings at the local disco and the desire to be shockingly, yet shabbily, glamourous throughout. More than any other band, they capture the desperation, the clumsiness, the whole chipped nail polish quality of the Seventies, and have gloriously dragged the entire sensibility

bang, slap into the middle of the Nineties. Without harbouring the merest trace of revivalism, Pulp have hung onto the ultra-humanness of a decade which couldn't be saved by the airbrush.

Unlike many a lesser band, Pulp have done far more to infuse the pop scene with a dash of Britain's saucy past than could be exhibited on a catwalk. Yes, their fashion sense is a crucial element, but even more so is Jarvis Cocker's lyrical view of life. Emotionally stunted, by his own admission, Jarvis believes his development instinctively halted at the dawn of the Eighties, which was, contrary to the opinion of style writer Peter York, a thoroughly dismal decade.

"When you got to the Eighties everyone started going Laura Ashley and everything started looking like *'Diary Of An Edwardian Lady'*." the singer told Gareth Grundy in a London Student interview. **"The emphasis on material things, the surface look of things, the shiny Porsche and the lovely grey leather sofa. It didn't matter about content."** he complained to the *Telegraph magazine*, while informing *Sky magazine* that **"the Seventies was the last future-looking period."**

Summing it all up to Select magazine, he said **"For me, the attraction of the Seventies is that it**

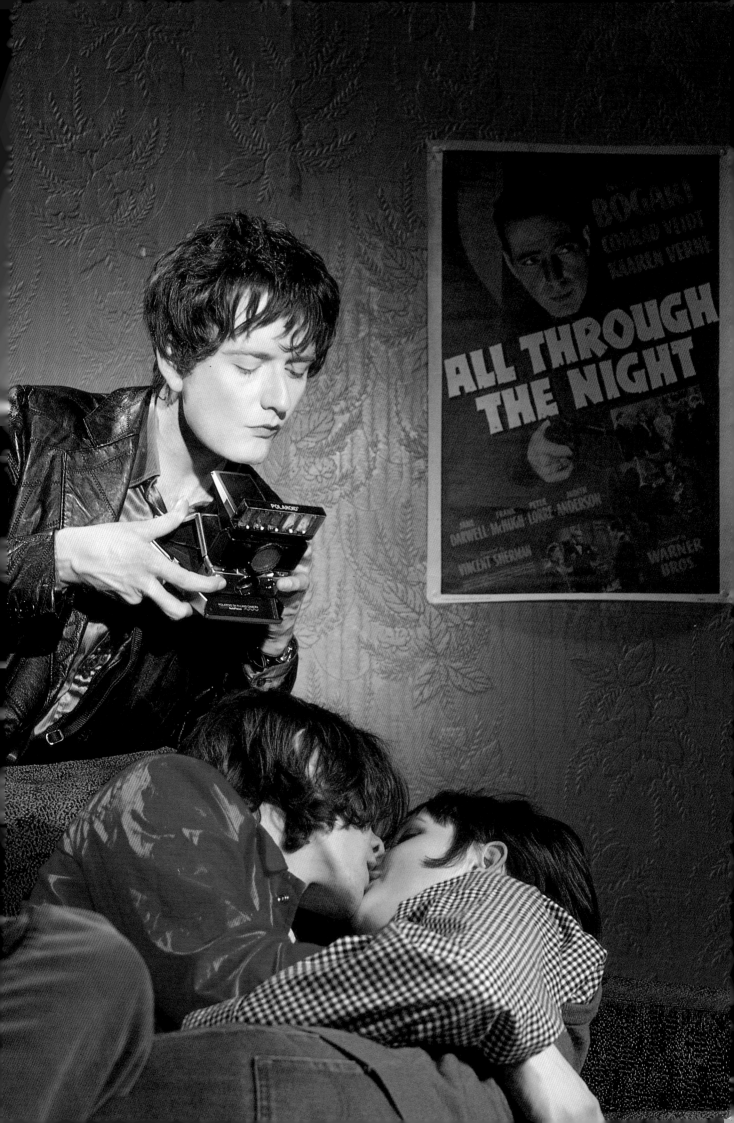

was a bit off, a bit eccentric, a bit wrong. Music and fashion and culture became stupidly exaggerated and then eventually imploded. But for all the silliness it was the last decade in which people did try and improve society. The Eighties were a nightmare from that point of view."

Film is a subject Jarvis knows a thing or two about, and he noticed the reflection of the Eighties' attitude on the movie industry. Two of Cocker's favourite directors, Ken Loach and Mike Leigh, were largely ignored in the Eighties, which was a decade when, as Jarvis put it, **"People wanted Merchant Ivory and Brideshead Revisited."**

ocker's songs share the bittersweet views of Leigh and Loach films. Unlike the illusory sets of Merchant Ivory productions, they are littered with disastrous and awkward liaisons, sinister obsessions and sexual weirdness, all wrapped up in some very real ugliness. You can feel the ghastly, lurid geometrical wallpaper peeling off behind the G-Plan, the stained pink, orange and brown nylon bedsheets catching at fingernails, and the static emanating from quilted, floral housecoats in his songs. Each one is illuminated by strip lights and scented with Hi Karate, Charlie, fried food and HP Sauce while relating some unbearable tale of the most unromantic order.

Jarvis understands that romance did not exist in Seventies Britain. Sex did, oh yes. But romance never went further than Milk Tray adverts.

"It was chicken in the basket and shagging in

the back of a car." he continued to Grundy, **"The Seventies were like, full of kids who'd go to the ice rink wearing flares and a straggly haircut. I remember when I was young there was a lot more sex on TV. There was more freedom, there was that feeling of people sitting in purple living rooms, shagging each other's wives. Supposedly glamourous, but a little bit sick in some ways."**

Such a frayed vision could only have sprouted from the experience of a Briton.

"How can you get into Route 66 when you live off the M1?" asked a bemused Jarvis of Miranda Sawyer in *The Observer's Life magazine.*

In America, the Great Dream glosses over the dirt coating the sidewalks, and consequently nobody bothers to address it, preferring to sing of blue skies, hot summer nights and pink Cadillacs. Even grunge found magnificence in gloom.

Speaking to Select, Jarvis explained **"When British pop is great it's because of the personality behind the music. The sense of the romantic in the everyday. Ray Davies finding the poetic in watching the sun go down over Waterloo station. You don't get that in much American rock."**

"Americans can quite happily write a song about Seattle, or some crappy little American town, and mean it and be serious, and elevate their own surroundings to a certain kind of drama." Russell Senior pointed out to David Bennun in a Melody Maker interview, expressing a slightly different take on things, **"But English**

people have to be self-deprecating."

"People think of suburbia as very boring but in a way it's quite exotic." said Jarvis by way of contrast, to Simon Price, again for *Melody Maker.* **"Some very strange things happen in these places."**

To illustrate his point, Jarvis goes on to relate how an old school chum had set up his own porn racket behind Sheffield's net curtains, filming himself having sex with various women in his own home, and flogging the tapes in local pubs.

"It was horrible." Jarvis spluttered, having been made to watch one in a house on a cul-de-sac, much to his disgust, **"Badly lit, the camera was shaking and you could just see this pink Draylon headboard all the time. And he had a tattoo on each buttock, These twisted little private lives are going on every day of the week."**

To *Attitude magazine* he said **"Where I lived there was a bloke who dressed as a man on the top half and a woman on the bottom half, wearing pleated skirts, women's' walking brogues and American tan tights. And there was my Uncle Ralph who lived across the road, who used to sit in his window with a German helmet on, listening to the Russian radio, playing his accordion, and more. Maybe because it is quite a bland uninspiring place to live, people invent little lives for themselves."**

COMMON PEOPLE

Without these little lives playing themselves out like curious and sometimes smutty disco-beat records, Jarvis would be short on song-worthy material. Building on a quintessentially English tradition of what Ian Penman has described as the *"Eng Lit hit"*, thus following on from the likes of Ray Davies, Kevin Ayers, Pete Townshend, Elvis Costello, (the American) Chrissie Hynde, Madness and the Pet Shop Boys, Jarvis deals in witty levellers, evocative summations of social scenes and situations. He also uses songs to poke fun at people who believe themselves to be above such things. Combining *"a very precise way with language and a very off-hand way with a regional accent"* as Penman has put it, Jarvis skillfully reproduces the ambience of ordinary Britain, using his own personality and physical extraordinariness to back up his tales. And while it's undoubtedly an act of sorts, it's one based on a premise of nothing more than obsessive observation - that healthy British pastime responsible for making suburbia's net curtains tweak so loudly.

"Nobody is making a conscious effort to be English," he maintained in *I-D magazine*, of the British pop scene in general, **"If you've been honest, if what you've been doing reflects what you're like as a person, it's inevitable that what you do is English."**

Pulp's *'Sheffield Sex City'* certainly reflected the band's Englishness. Released towards the end of 1992, it provided a sonic trawl round *"the fleshpots of Sheffield in a T-reg Chevette"* according to Jarvis. Wybourn, Attercliffe, Wincobank, Brincliffe, Intake and other such heaving Northern Sodoms and Gomorrahs featured in the tune which also included a fine piece of detail from Candida Doyle about listening to next door's private activities through a thin flat wall.

Talking to Select's Adam Higginbotham, Jarvis confessed that coming from England didn't automatically make you a fan of your own country, it merely meant that you resigned yourself to your roots. In turn, this produced a healthy amount of criticism.

"I've been sick of Britain for as long as I can remember, but you have to accept that it's where you come from. The things that are good about it are the things that criticise it. There's a thriving counterculture here because mass culture is so bad."

Purveyors and relayers of a great British vision, albeit a far from traditional one, Pulp are undoubtedly among the finest exponents of contemporary English pop. Jarvis deplores patriotic jingoism, has no time for football hooligans or the typical Brit abroad (who decries foreigners and their food) admires Arthur Scargill, hates Americanisms like *'I'll write you'* as opposed to the correct *'I'll write to you'* and loves chips, Scotland, the Peak district and cul-de-sac culture. You can hear it all jostling about in his songs. Together with tarnished memories of Flintlock and glitter balls. It's like the Eighties and grunge never happened. ●

I WILL SURVIVE

SURVIVE

- THE LONG

& WINDING

HISTORY

OF PULP

"I'd spent the best part of a decade in bed and in an unsuccessful band"

I WILL SURVIVE

nlike many of today's British pop bands, Pulp did not enjoy a sudden rise to success. They were not groomed for stardom in their tender years, nor were they bound for the fast route to fame. Far from it. Pulp were something like 16 years in the making, and for that alone they deserve respect and recognition. Most musicians who'd been dealt their kind of luck would have given up aeons ago.

Eternal oddball, Jarvis Cocker, always knew he wanted to be a star. If he was a star he'd have something tangible to focus his freakiness on. People wouldn't laugh at him anymore because he'd simply get away with it. Be admired for it even. He knew it was the only feasible route to follow, and besides, imagining that he and his friends were in a pop group made life so much more exciting. So one day at school, in the middle of an economics lesson, he founded Pulp. Arabicus Pulp, to be exact. Wayne Furniss was appointed to play drums (and still does, with a Sheffield band called The Absolute), Jamie Pinchbeck opted for bass and Pete Dalton

I WILL SURVIVE

provided guitars and synthesiser. Jarvis, of course, sang and wrote lyrics.

'Arabicus' was taken from the *Financial Times*, and was a commodity of some description, although Jarvis can't remember what exactly. And Jarvis had always wanted 'Pulp', so Arabicus Pulp they were. They played a couple of gigs, but then decided to drop the 'Arabicus' bit because it took too long to say.

n their early days, the band played cover versions of Motorhead's interpretation of *'Leavin' Here'* by Holland-Dozier-Holland, *'The House Of The Rising Sun'* by The Animals and *'Wild Thing'*. They also made some Super-8 films including The Three Spartans and Spaghetti Western Meets Star Trek, which starred the 17 year old Jarvis as Clint Eastwood. At one of their gigs in a small upstairs room at Sheffield's Hallamshire, two girls wrapped them up in toilet rolls as they played, but one of them lost her footing and fell off the stage, injuring her ankle, much to the amusement of the audience. Their gigs, it would seem, were always something of a spectacle.

In 1981, Pulp made their first demo with Ken Patten, and ended up being invited to Maida Vale in London to record a session for John Peel. The producer, Dale Griffin, was apparently outraged by the drumkit, which was pieced together from a burglar alarm and a calculator, but somehow the

session was completed and Jarvis returned to Sheffield looking forward to his new life of fame and fortune as a pop star.

Unfortunately, no record companies came flocking, the rest of the band jacked in all hope of ever appearing on Top Of The Pops, and, giving into parental pressures, departed for university.

Dalton's father, a teacher, was especially severe about his son's future.

"He over-reacted, he threw his dinner at him." Jarvis recalled in an interview with Stuart Maconie for Select, "In the end the others went their own way. Pulp was just me and I had to find a new band."

Dalton is now a priest.

Jarvis's next stab at fame arrived in the shape of an audition to present The Tube. Sadly he failed at that too. Fame was evidently keeping its distance.

In 1983, Pulp reformed with Simon Hinkler, later

of The Mission, as part of the line-up. Hinkle has since produced the band. In fact "He did a lot of work for Pulp but he doesn't like to talk about it." according to Russell Senior.

By now the band even had a manager, Tony Perrin, who went on to form Golden Dawn management who handled The Mission and All About Eve during the Eighties. (Perrin currently takes care of indie band Nilon Bombers and also looked after

Flying Medallions before one of their members was tragically killed in a tourbus crash in 1995.)

This Pulp incarnation lasted through the recording of the debut album, 'It', but again crumbled when success still refused to put in an appearance.

In 1984, Jarvis decided to follow the path he forsook after school, and made plans to read English at Liverpool University. But he ran into guitarist and violinist Russell Senior, a business studies graduate with a neat little line in antique dealing, who'd first spotted Jarvis during his fishmongering days, and remembered him for his saucy market speak.

"Even then the sexual innuendos were there." he recalled.

Senior's own trading days were pretty standard by comparison. **"I never made any money, although the stuff I used to sell is all the rage now."** he said to *Impact*, **"Used to sell it for a tenner, now it goes for thousands. I think my heart was somewhere else."**

For Jarvis, hooking up with Senior meant that Liverpool suddenly looked a little less enticing next to the reawakened prospect of stardom, and the English books stayed on the shelf while he headed back to the rehearsal rooms.

Senior met Pulp the band, as opposed to Jarvis the Cocker, while he was interviewing them for his fanzine, *The Bath Banker*. He had also written a play for Jarvis called *The Fruits of Passion* in which the singer was depicted eating (fake) dog excrement. **"It was Dadaist - kind of Zurich 1919 revolutionary...the idea was to provoke."** he explained to Impact.

With Senior's services, Pulp recorded their second album, 'Freaks', and played a number of ill received shows. **"Everybody thought it was a very good comedy act: where we were trying to be Cabaret Voltaire or something and everybody else thought we were The Krankies."** Senior recalled to *Impact,* **"The more pissed off we got, the higher the level of comedy to the audience, and we're thinking 'No, no, we're all misunderstood.'...You used to spend more time making sure the slide projector was working and not tripping over all the kak all over the stage than bothering to tune our instruments."**

Drummer Magnus Doyle used to trash his kit at the end of each song, and had to quickly put it all back together again before the next one started (another drummer once spun round on his seat so fast he flew off, and needless to say, never played with the band again). According to Jarvis all the fans were *"mentally unbalanced"* and The Smiths were driving him insane with jealousy, because they were just beginning to take off.

And that's when Jarvis fell 30 feet from a window.

Up until this point, Jarvis had been living in an old steel factory next to rehearsal rooms, two tennis clubs and surrounded by loads of crazy Sheffield people including a model railway enthusiast. He began to worry about himself, about how

marginalised he was feeling, and the *'Freaks'* album summed it all up. **"I was worried that I was turning into a freak."** he calmly informed Select's Stuart Maconie.

His accident helped him to put things into perspective a little bit, but he continued with Pulp, performing in a wheelchair until he was healed. Sadly fate was not on his side, despite his remarkable recovery from injuries which doctors believed would leave him a cripple. Bottles were thrown at his band by upset rugby players, and people just didn't get them. Maybe it had something to do with the bloke that used to pop up between songs to read out poetry and let off his factory siren. Apparently, he once blew up all the fuses in the building and Pulp had to wait 20 minutes before they could continue with their set.

The last straw arrived with the conversion of their bass player, Anthony, to a local Christian cult. Anthony had always been a bit partial to LSD, and so his mind was slightly scrambled, making him more susceptible to crazy ideas about Jesus. Famous for taking his clothes off at the end of each Pulp set, he left to go gadding about with the rave vicar who caused such a sensation in 1995, but resurfaced during Elastica's performance at the 25th Glastonbury Festival, romping about the stage stark naked. By then he'd put Jesus and the rave vicar

Something changed for Pulp as they collected their long awaited awards - Javis and Eva Herzigova at the MTV Music Awards '95 (left) and Jarvis at the Brit Awards

nonsense firmly behind him, but evidently hadn't forgotten about drugs. Apparently he'd spent the day of his stage frolics waltzing around the festival site dressed as George Best.

With so much weirdness around him, Jarvis began to feel like his life might just never happen. So he decided to go to college. He'd begun to lose it himself a bit, and had started collecting things from jumble sales and stuffing them into bags which he never opened, scattering them around his room. When he started to have trouble opening the door because of all the clutter in the way, he realised he'd better do something - fast. Or else he'd end up like all the other has-been musos, who wandered about town looking like lost dogs.

"I'd spent the best part of a decade in bed and

in an unsuccessful group," he told Maconie in *Select*, **"I was forced to admit I'd been wasting my time. It was humiliating."**

Going to college in London at least gave Jarvis a sense of direction, and he put the band to sleep for a while. New bass player Steve Mackey was at college with him, and the other three, Senior, keyboard player Candida Doyle (Magnus's sister) and drummer Nick Banks stayed in Sheffield. They managed to meet up every other month or so to rehearse, and even played the odd gig, but their life as a band was barely ticking.

Ironically enough, it was during this period that Pulp's popularity really started to catch on. So, in 1988, they decided to give it one last try.

"When we relaunched in 1988, it was kind of

'Well...we could call it Pulp'." said Senior to *Impact*, explaining why the band kept their original name, "**It wasn't automatic but people knew the name. It was a different line-up but there was some continuity. We'd probably have become famous quicker if we'd come out as a new band, cos people thought; 'God, they've been going for years. If they were any good they would've got signed by now.'"**

n truth their name seemed immaterial. All of a sudden, press and public alike were sitting up and taking notice of the spindly boy with the clumsy co-ordination and his bizarre band. The music press became aware of their existence, thanks to their new publicist, Melissa Thompson of Savage and Best (who initially toiled over their campaigns for free, on the understanding that Pulp would pay the company back once they'd made their mark, and who has since won awards for her work with them) and somehow their peculiar style and distinctive sound caught on. It was almost a matter of timing - a question of sticking it out and letting the rest of the world catch up with them.

"**We could never split up because we never had the definitive answer...because we never had any exposure.**" Senior told *Impact*, "**No matter how good we thought Pulp were, we would have been really happy to pack this thing in if we thought nobody else liked it. But we did have this sneaking suspicion...**"

These days Pulp have an added guitarist, Mark Webber, originally a fan who first saw them perform while Jarvis was still confined to his wheelchair. Their singles are guaranteed to be hits, and they have acquired a large enough fanbase to fill an entire tour of Britain's arenas.

"**I wasn't surprised when they finally became successful.**" said Martin Lacey, editor of Sheffield's *NMX fanzine* and Pulp expert, speaking to the *Sheffield Telegraph* in 1995, "**But I did tend to think that they would be one of those always undiscovered geniuses like Cabaret Voltaire and Wreckless Eric, who would just eventually vanish from the scene.**"

"**But these things come round. The music business is always looking for something to sell and they just thought 'we'll try Pulp'. It wasn't that Pulp had been any different for all those years, it's just that the music industry chose to ignore them.**"

Hard to imagine anybody ignoring Pulp really, especially when you consider the amount of attention their singer used to command just by walking down the street at the age of nine. The difference of course, is that back then he was noticed for all the wrong reasons.

"**It's what I always wanted, right back to that time when I felt I was marginalised.**" commented Jarvis, speaking about his new-found star status to Q's David Quantick, now his moment of triumph had finally arrived. "**It makes you feel that you haven't wasted 15 years of your life, that you were right to have carried on. It makes you feel that you weren't mentally ill all that time.**" ●

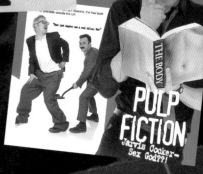

VERSACE VS CANCER RESEARCH - THE PECULIAR SENSE OF PULP FASHION

"I used to go shopping with my mother dressed as Batman"

ulp are renowned for their glamour. They ooze sparkle and shine, they drip pazazz and they give off glitz like royalty. Goddammit - they've even been known to glide down the odd catwalk. It wasn't always like this though. Beneath Jarvis Cocker's shimmering suits there lies the body of a pool cue, and while its possessor has preened himself beyond geek-abberation to become a much sought after sex symbol, having a badly behaved fashion sense has certainly helped.

Jarvis has never been exactly what you'd call an orthodox dresser. When he was a seven year old child, his mother sent him to school looking like *"an extra from Heidi"* thanks to a German relation who used to send over pairs of lederhosen.

"I managed to cajole my grandma into buying me some normal shorts and I'd change on the way to school." he told Amy Raphael of *The Face,*

"People would generally call me names and think I was odd."

He also had very long hair, which his mother neglected to cut, and combined with his long, skinny body, his short shorts and long jumpers (which gave the appearance of a dress) and his great big National Health spectacles, he looked incredibly peculiar indeed.

"I was the only boy on the street with long hair," he confessed to Q's Andrew Collins, **"People used to think I was a girl which caused me no end of embarrassment. I had long blond hair and little round glasses and I looked like the Milky Bar kid."**

Jarvis also harboured a keen desire to be Batman, and it is to this early dressing up period that he owes his adult fascination for costume and glamour.

"My mum made me a cape," he told *I-D magazine,* **"I wore some purple tights and I had a Batman mask. I used to go shopping with my mother dressed as Batman."**

As a child, Jarvis maintains he desperately wanted to fit in. He didn't enjoy looking so freakish, being sent to school resembling an *"Alpine shepherd boy"* and constantly getting mistaken for a girl.

"I never wanted to be different," he insisted to Ben Thompson for *The Independent,* **"I wanted to be the same. I just wanted to wear shorts that were vaguely near the knee rather than somewhere up here (meaning the top of his thighs)".**

But when punk exploded in the mid-Seventies, he

suddenly decided that it was all right to be different, and began his current pattern of exaggerating his individuality. To begin with, he was probably a little clumsy about it. He used to go to gigs wearing crocheted ties.

"I used to wear my Dad's Sixties suits, three sizes too big." he said in the *Telegraph magazine*, **" I dyed a pair of my grandad's shoes turquoise with Lady Esquire shoe dye and had pink laces in them - stuff like that."** He said he was never beaten up exactly, although admitted that looking different makes people want to beat you up because they think you're queer. **"I once got a kebab pushed into my face with quite a lot of force on a late-night bus."**

"I realised early on that I could never look like the other kids, because I was too tall, so I thought if they're going to take the piss anyway, I might as well accentuate it, rather than stoop and pretend not to be tall. "** he related to Simon Price of *Melody Maker*, **"You 'ave to turn it into a fashion feature. But I think I'm stylish."** He then went on to indicate the very plush dark fake fur coat he was wearing, which apparently had belonged to his grandad to illustrate his point. **"I've had it for ten years. I never wear things for a** joke, but I suppose it makes walking down the street a bit more of an adventure."**

Determined to exaggerate his elongated, gawky physique, Jarvis stepped out of the shadows and took on a whole new air of confidence - one which helped to keep him going through the years of pre-success Pulp.

"I really do believe that you should exaggerate your supposedly bad features." he declared to Melody Maker's Stud Brothers, **"You know, if you've got big feet wear big shoes, if you're tall and skinny wear very tight clothes. If there is something odd about you then you either consign yourself to the margins or play on your uniqueness."**

"Obviously it's got to do with the way you carry yourself. I mean there are certain people who wouldn't feel comfortable overstating what they have spent years trying to conceal. It's like when you're naked you know. Some people stand there looking really vulnerable and they withdraw into themselves. Other people just look like they couldn't give a fuck what anyone thinks."

Jarvis believes he belongs to the latter category. After battling with the lederhosen he evidently developed an in-built survival mechanism which meant that no matter how badly his stringbean body was attired, he wouldn't crumble. Wearing normal clothes did nothing to hide his angular proportions, so he decided to go the whole hog. Having the piss taken out of him was hardly a new experience, and anyway, as he so rightly observed, once you declare

yourself to be a clear and away inimitable individual, you start attracting like-minded or like-bodied people.

"There's these two mates of mine who dressed weirdly and they met while being chased by skinheads. They're best mates now. So it does act like a sign."

Pulp's highly original Oxfam look has its roots in this attitude of Jarvis's. As a teenager he wore his grandad's and dad's cast-offs, but he soon began hunting down bargains in local charity shops and still shops in places like Freak Boutique, on Sheffield's Division Street, which specialises in Seventies clothing - surprisingly enough.

"The last thing I bought there was a pink and purple patterned shirt." he informed the NME in April 1993, "Sheffield's pretty good for second hand clothes. The jumble sales are best because they're the purest form - you don't know what you'll get, the clothes haven't been sifted."

"If you've bought something and it only cost 20p you can experiment and throw it away if you don't like it." he added in the *Telegraph magazine.*

"Jarvis was always finding shades of mustard that others never knew existed." recalled Russell Senior of his frontman's jumble-hunt days.

This second hand clothing sensibility earned Pulp - and in particular Jarvis - some rather undecided reactions during their early gigging days.

"I REALLY DO BELIEVE THAT YOU SHOULD EXAGGERATE YOUR SUPPOSEDLY BAD FEATURES"

"The singer wins my nomination for any snappy dresser of the month award going, psychedelically tasteless in faded pink trousers, pukey green shirt, suede jacket, glasses and dorky non-hairdo."

wrote Martin Lacey in Sheffield's *NMX fanzine* in 1981, in a review of the band's gig at the Royal Hotel on Abbeydale Road. These days, Lacey edits NMX and owns Juma Print which is based in Sheffield's Wellington Street, the press responsible for producing Pulp People's fan club material.

"They never fitted any trend and they never jumped on any band wagon," he told the *Sheffield Telegraph* 14 years after his review. **"They were awkward and unmarketable, unglamorous, hype-free. But persistence paid off."**

Indeed it did. And not just in the musical sense. At the beginning of 1993, *Select magazine* hailed Pulp as the Kings of Crimplenism, alongside Denim, Suede and Saint Etienne. Fashion wise - they had officially arrived in the effervescent world of pop.

Having struck out in life as a loping, geek-u-like, with dodgy haircuts and equally questionable face furniture, Jarvis now features in fashion magazines, attends Versace parties, and shuffles down catwalks. The heavy specs have been discarded for contacts, his typically Eighties bush-curl has been tamed into a sleek, although slightly tousled crop, and even his jumble sale hunts are being traded in for free designer pieces.

"Are you ever off duty fashion-wise?" enquired journalist Miranda Sawyer for an interview with *The*

VERSACE Vs CANCER RESEARCH

Observer's Life magazine. **"No."** came the reply, **"I'm on call 24 hours a day. Like a doctor."** He informed **Just 17 magazine that his favourite colour was pink - "Not many men can get away with it 'cos they think it's effeminate, but I can get away with it."**

And he declared to Andrew Smith of The Face that his most treasured possession was his shoes. - **"I've got about 50 pairs. I'm known as the Imelda Marcos of Yorkshire. They're my favourite things and in any town I go to, I'll always go hunting for shoes. I really like them. Even women's shoes."**

When asked by Select's Adam Higginbotham what the best item of clothing he'd bought in 1993 was, he answered **"These shoes."** Higginbotham described them as *"chisel-toed burgundy loafers with square buckles"* and Jarvis went on to say **"They've a kind of highwayman look to them. They were in a charity shop in Mornington Crescent. Very well made. Made in Italy. I was after a more Regency look and they're helping me to get my way."**

In June of 1995, Jarvis's shoe fetish reached an all-time high when he took to the catwalk for a charity fashion show at London's Saatchi Gallery. Modelling a pair of shoes specially designed for him by second-year college student Cordelia Vanman from the Cordwainers College of Shoe Design in London, he stole the show by creaking down the aisle with a walking stick, pretending to be an octogenarian. The shiny, baby blue shoes featured a transparent upper, and fetched £5,100 for War Child, the charity set up to benefit Croatian and Bosnian children. Brian Eno organised the event, which raised a total of £50,000, with Jarvis's shoes fetching the top bid.

Select went one step further when they asked Jarvis to imagine his own clothing line. He mused over calling it Jarvgear and decided it would be a great idea because as he'd only produce clothes in his size, he'd never have trouble shopping again.

Despite his love of the garish and the gauche, Jarvis maintains that he would never wear something as a joke. In fact, the very notion of 'kitsch' appals him, implying, as it does, a potentially damaging lack of seriousness.

"Although in retrospect I may look at something I wore and regret it," he told the *NME*, **"I know I thought it was worthwhile at the time. And I hate the words 'kitsch' and 'ironic'. Loathe them. They're nothing to do with what me or Pulp are about. I haven't devoted 15 years of my life to a joke."**

Indeed, if Jarvis was an ironic joke, top designers would hardly be flocking to him with requests for him to wear their clothes. It wouldn't exactly make for good publicity.

"I've got a meeting with Katherine Hamnett and I've managed to get Gucci to send me some shoes." he coolly uttered to the *Telegraph magazine* in 1995, **"I do think there are some quite good clothes designers around at the moment."** ●

LET THE BEAT GO ON
- THE WORDS AND MUSIC OF PULP

"I used to get in loads of trouble
with girls I went out with because they
thought I was a bastard for writing
about them"

estering away in the mind of its strange creator, who grew increasingly frustrated as time ticked away, at one point it looked as if no one beyond the cold, grey borders of Sheffield would ever hear Jarvis Cocker's witticisms and the band's quirky pop rhythms.

Then suddenly it all exploded. Pulp had a hit. In 1995, *'Common People'* climbed to number two in the British charts, held back from the top spot only by America's monstrous advertisement for why no one should ever have plastic surgery - Michael Jackson, who with sister Janet had a number one with *'Scream'*. At last Pulp were famous. Really famous.

Pop-star-of-the-highest-order-famous. And not just because they liked spangly clothes.

It all started with a Peel session 15 years ago. The band Jarvis Cocker had put together while still at school, had made a demo with an elderly chap called Ken Patten who'd set up some studio equipment in his home.

"You recorded in his bedroom and he had closed-circuit television to see you weren't messing around." Jarvis told Record Collector.

Patten claimed to be the inventor of the Vocoder, a device favoured by the Electric Light Orchestra no less, although his version involved toilet rolls, ancient throat microphones and synthesisers - and only cost 50p.

Despite such lack of technical sophistication, Pulp managed to record four tracks, and when John Peel arrived in Sheffield with his road show, Jarvis summoned up the guts to give him a copy.

All of this resulted in the much sought after session, but although Peel later revealed that he thought the recordings which included *'Turkey Mambo Momma'*, *'Wishful Thinking'*, *'Refuse To Be Blind'* and *'Please Don't Worry'* were pretty good for a band who hadn't had much gigging or studio experience, he didn't offer them another slot until 1994.

John Peel's intervention, albeit ultimately fruitless, was enough to persuade Jarvis to leave school and

concentrate on his band. The Peel session inspired Statik's Nigel Burnham to ask them for a track for his compilation, *'Your Secret's Safe With Us'*, which appeared in 1982. Pulp willingly supplied *'What Do You Say'* from their Patten demo, but soon afterwards the band fell apart, leaving Jarvis to go forth and invoke another incarnation.

Blissfully unaware that he was to spend the next

14 years or so desperately trying to keep his head above water, he struck out on a long and winding road, found new members and recorded his first single in April of 1983 for Red Rhino records. Titled *'My Lighthouse'*, it was a fey, whimsical acoustic number inspired by the lighthouse dweller in the movie, *'Diva'*. This was followed by *'Everybody's Problem'* two months later, a song which heralded

the downfall of Pulp Mark Two. Having been informed by his then manager to come up with a Wham type tune, Jarvis penned in a disastrous brass section, refused to sing properly at the recording, and generally messed up bigtime.

By now, Pulp had also recorded their first mini album. 'It' appeared in August 1983, again on Red Rhino. Jarvis claimed it was inspired by Leonard Cohen, complete with female backing vocals and acoustic instruments and when Cherry Red re-released it 11 years later on CD, he was pleasantly surprised.

"It's quite sophisticated," he said, while simultaneously admitting it embarrassed him, **"It's full of love songs, but from the perspective of not knowing about it."**

Despite a positive reception, the album didn't quite take off, and while similarly inclined artists like Tracey Thorn and the Marine Girls went on to enjoy success, Pulp collapsed for the second time.

Not to be dissuaded easily, Jarvis pressed on, and a year later resurfaced with a new line up, and a new single about a girl who gets pregnant, written after seeing a picture of his mother stepping out of her wedding car at the tender age of 20. Issued in December 1985 by Fire records, the label who were to tarnish Pulp's career for years to come, *'Little Girl (With Blue Eyes)'* was well received, but didn't enjoy any radio airplay.

Around this time, Jarvis got into easy listening. He said he needed something to calm him down, and besides, he was fed up with modern music, partly because the success of his contemporaries merely served to remind him of his own comparative failure. So he soothed himself with the likes of Henry Mancini and Burt Bacharach, and battled on in the hope of making it.

une 1986 saw the release of the *'Dogs Are Everywhere'* EP, the title track of which was inspired by *"the doggish attitude"* of people who get pissed and steal things. Also featured were *'Mark Of The Devil'*, an earnest attempt at disco-beat music, *'97 Lovers'* about an auntie who had a huge poster of a scantily clad Roger Moore above her bed, *'Aborigine'* about a man who grows fat while waiting for his life to begin, and *'Goodnight'*, a *"concept piece which sounded like falling asleep."* Melody Maker awarded the EP Single Of The Week.

That month Pulp also began recording their 'Freaks (Ten Songs About Power, Claustrophobia, Suffocation And Holding Hands)' album. Released in May 1987 and made for the grand sum of £600, it was eventually disowned by the producer.

For Jarvis, things were now taking an especially bad turn. The songs, in his opinion, were fine, just

badly done, but even if they'd been performed and recorded immaculately, they were so far away from chart-busting material, that they wouldn't have stood a chance anyway.

'They Suffocate At Night', another single, was also released in June 1986, followed by 'Masters Of The Universe', taken from 'Freaks' in March 1987. The latter featured B sides including a reworking of Serge Gainsbourg's 'Manon', plus a horrendous drone called 'Silence', which Jarvis banned from reappearing on the 'Masters Of The Universe' compilation album of 1994, because it was so excruciating.

By this point, Pulp's relationship with Fire records had deteriorated so badly that they began recording with Fon records in Sheffield. 'Don't You Want Me Anymore', 'Rattlesnakes', and 'Death Comes To Town' all show Pulp in full Eurodisco mode, but sadly none of them were ever released, despite being, in Jarvis's opinion, the band's best recordings to date.

Thoroughly disillusioned, Jarvis upped and offed to London, re-linked up with Fire (bad move, but

nobody else seemed interested) and began work on the *'Separations'* album. *'My Legendary Girlfriend'* was the first single to emerge from the recordings, and was written about the relationship Jarvis had had in Sheffield. Apparently he'd never taken his girlfriend out, not being one to combine his personal life with his musical existence, so she'd taken on a legendary status for being completely invisible.

It was at this stage that Fire records really began to mess Pulp about. *'My Legendary Girlfriend'* didn't appear until September 1990, ten months after *'Separations'* was finished. Still NME dubbed it Single Of The Week, and finally Pulp's popularity started to swell.

The album continued to be frustratingly on hold, but *'Countdown'* was issued in August 1991. This time the theme was waiting for life to get going, while the actual countdown to the big moment never happened - a feeling Jarvis was all too familiar with.

Finally, *'Separations'* saw the light of day in October 1991. It was the last time Pulp worked with the label, and lots of bitter feelings were flying around. Jarvis negotiated a happier deal with Gift, a sister label to Warp and the single *'O.U.'* was released in May 1992.

Called *'O.U.'* because it sounded like the theme

tune to Open University, the song was about **"a man faced with the decision of hearing his girlfriend leaving him, and it's only eight o'clock in the morning, and he has to decide whether he wants to stay in bed for an extra hour, or get dressed and go and stop her leaving him forever."**

Melody Maker made it Single Of The Week 2 ,and elsewhere it received mixed reviews from the British music press, who mused over the *'weird keyboards'* and thrilled over the achingly real-life lyrics.

'Babies' followed on five months later, and was hailed as the Best New Single in Smash Hits. Its confusing storyline baffled many a pop critic, and all kinds of modified versions were related in the reviews, but the actual tale is about a boy who has a crush on a female friend and goes to her house after school where he hides in her older sister's wardrobe and watches her having sex with the kid from the garage down the road. One day she discovers him so they get it on, and his friend (who he really fancies) discovers them. In the end he admits he only did it 'cos the older sister looked like her younger sibling!

Things were definitely on an upward spiral for Pulp now. Their next single, *'Razzmatazz'* was favourably received by both Melody Maker and NME, despite being the **"most bitter song we've ever done."** according to Jarvis, who also admitted that

"however harsh I am about the people in 'Razzmatazz', I'm not writing from above their level. I've got a lot of experience of being just as sad as them, if not more so."

hen I first met Jarvis I embarrassed him by saying I thought 'Razzmatazz' was a work of utter genius."** said Jo Brand during an interview with Johnny Dee for the *NME,* in which she and Jarvis were both featured. **"I like Jarvis's songs because he realises that life is basically shit, but it's OK."**

The national tabloid, *The Daily Star*, reported that Jarvis was hoping it would be a hit so he could buy himself a telephone.

The B side - *'Inside Susan: A Story in 3 Parts'* also intrigued more than one journalist. Written over three songs, it was based on two real people, neither of whom were called Susan, and traced the life of a girl through from her adolescence to her thirties. First seen at a bus stop wearing an alluring halter-top and a blue trainer bra, she ends up in an uncomfortably comfortable marriage to an architect.

The final part, *'59 Lyndhurst Grove'* was inspired by a party Jarvis had been thrown out of by an architect (of course). Jarvis later said the party was awful, being full of the politically correct middle classes and their kids, and when he'd recorded the song he sent a CD copy to the architect's wife. He never heard from her, but apparently a Japanese fan turned up on the family's doorstep, demanding to know whether the Mrs was actually Susan.

PULP. HIS 'N' HERS.

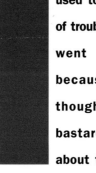 used to get in loads of trouble with girls I went out with because they thought I was a bastard for writing about them," Jarvis told Ben Thompson of *The Independent*, relating the trouble telling true life tales can land a body in, **"and I don't blame them. Especially when I wouldn't even tell them the things I was talking about in the songs to their faces."**

The legal minefield surrounding Pulp and Fire records was still sending up explosions, but Island were about to come to the rescue. In September of 1993, champagne bottles were uncorked, and Pulp inked their first major label deal, much to their relief. At last they could move into decent accommodation, stop fretting over the bills and pay for their own drinks at night-clubs.

The first Island single was *'Lipgloss'*, released in November 1993. Again, Jarvis provided the story behind the song. **"The title came from a story I heard about an anorexic girl who used to eat only lipgloss. And the rest of the song - about a girl who has her self confidence bashed down by a bad relationship - is based on someone I knew. I think it's important to express these stories so that victims know they're not the only ones suffering."**

And as if that wasn't enough to satisfy the reviewers, the video starred a girl who performed *"sexual art"* (as opposed to pornography).

The following April, the debut Island album was available. *'His'n'Hers'* was released to critical acclaim, after an erratic recording period. Wrapped in a glossy sleeve which featured an airbrush portrait of Pulp by top Seventies artist Philip Castle, the record was immediately eye-catching. **"I was surprised when they asked me to do it."** Philip told *Select magazine,* **"I think Jarvis and Steve felt that the look of my work enhanced what they were doing. It's heartening to be plunged back into the heart of popular culture."**

Recounting the studio sessions to Record Collector, Jarvis explained how strange happenings had plagued the band and Ed Buller, their producer, after they'd laid down a track called *'The Tunes Of Evil'*.

"The mixing desk blew up, the multi track for *'Joyriders'* (a song about a bunch of kids who ask to borrow the singer's Hillman Imp so they can take a girl to the reservoir) disintegrated and we had to piece it back together by clever jiggery pokery. Ed Buller developed strange pains in his back and generally, the vibe went bad."

'Tunes' as it had been known, was destroyed,

PULP. THE SISTERS EP.

PULP.
DO YOU REMEMBER
THE FIRST TIME ?

with the atmospheric music at the beginning of *'Acrylic Afternoons'* being the final product.

The first single release from *'His'n'Hers'* arrived in March 1994, and was *'Do You Remember The First Time?'*, the song for which Jarvis made a 30 minute film. Backed with *'The Babysitter'* in which Susan re-appears, it made number 33 in the charts.

"It's certainly quite a bitter song." Jarvis informed *The Crack* magazine, **"It got me thinking about the first time I had sex, and how when you're older you get quite blasé about it. Sex should be an intense and special thing. It's ridiculous how older people can get themselves involved in relationships where all there is, is sex, quite sad really."**

The accompanying film was a highly entertaining piece of work during which Jarvis described his own first time, which took place on a patch of grass near a bandstand in one of Sheffield's parks. It also featured Vic Reeves, Bob Mortimer, Jo Brand, Alison Steadman, Terry Hall, Elastica's Justine Frischmann, John Peel, Sir Viv Stanshall and Candida Doyle's mum, Sandra Woe (known for her appearances in Coronation Street and Mike Leigh films) all giving their personal accounts of defloration.

Then came the *'Three Sisters'* EP in May (also boasting a Philip Castle design - this time a Seventies' original of four hairstyles) which featured a re-release of *'Babies'*, plus *'Your Sister's Clothes'*, *'Seconds'* and *'His'n'Hers'*. Again exploring the theme of people settling for second best, it was a reflection on the situations of some of Jarvis's friends he'd left behind in Sheffield. **"It sometimes seemed the life of my contemporaries was like a marathon - who'd give up first. "** he said to *The Bath Chronicle*.

'Seconds' was to do with **"the idea of the 'second-hand' people who've been through the mill a bit."** while *'Your Sister's Clothes'* **"explores the ideas that perfect people are, well, perfectly boring to be honest."** *'Three Sisters'* charted at number 19, preparing the way for the super-success which was lurking just around the corner.

And so finally, lo and behold, a year later Pulp well and truly arrived with their next single, *'Common People'*. Inspired by a Greek girl Jarvis met while studying film at St. Martin's College in London, it spoke of the extremely patronising and unrealistic romantic myths spun around less well off people by the rich.

The girl was from a wealthy shipping family and decided that she'd quite like to live in some downtrodden area of the capital, like Hackney, because she wanted to suffer for her art - literally! Jarvis maintained that people from upper classes are fascinated and probably envious of the energy generated by poorer people, because it's something they'll never have. **"It's an energy which comes from desperation and rich people are never going to feel that"** he said to *Elle* magazine.

'Common People' was backed with *'Underwear'* a

| *'RUSSELL'* PATTERN NO. 9/1995 STYLE COMPONENT NO. **1** | *'JARVIS'* PATTERN NO. 9/1995 STYLE COMPONENT NO. **2** | *'MARK'* PATTERN NO. 9/1995 STYLE COMPONENT NO. **3** | *'STEVE'* PATTERN NO. 9/1995 STYLE COMPONENT NO. **4** |

look at the doubts you feel after getting home with someone you're not totally sure about - that moment when you have to decide whether or not to give into your most basic bodily urge, which leaves you feeling horribly out of control. (Jarvis likened it to giving into the kebab house when you're pissed. You know it'll make you feel bad, but you feel bad anyway so you figure you might as well make yourself feel worse.

"It's good to acknowledge that sometimes you get those unwise urges. Somehow from taking it that far, you get something out of it." he calmly told *The Face*.

"It's about being past the point of no return but not wanting to do anything," he told the *NME,* when *'Common People'* made Single of the Week, before unsurprisingly adding **"It's a bit personal."**

"I write about sex because I think it motivates people's actions a lot of the time." the singer told Amy Raphael in *The Face*, **"Not enough is written about the psychological dimension of it; that was**

what was hard for me at first, being quite reserved, being an inch away from someone."

uring one week in June the single sold no less than 70,000 copies. The huge success of *'Common People'* brought Pulp in from the cold of anonymity, to the warmth and sparkle of *'Top Of The Pops'*, top social class parties and the land of London's celebrities. It was all a far cry from the bitter wastes of Sheffield, and something the band have now become quite accustomed to, although as Jarvis has since remarked, **"My life now consists mostly of things I wouldn't want to write songs about."**

The double A-sided *'Sorted For E's And Whizz'* and *'Mis-Shapes'* was the subject of huge controversy

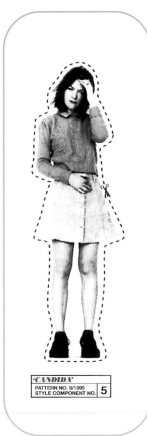

'CANDIDA'
PATTERN NO. 9/1995
STYLE COMPONENT NO. 5

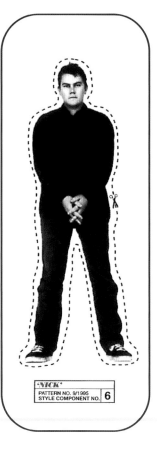

'NICK'
PATTERN NO. 9/1995
STYLE COMPONENT NO. 6

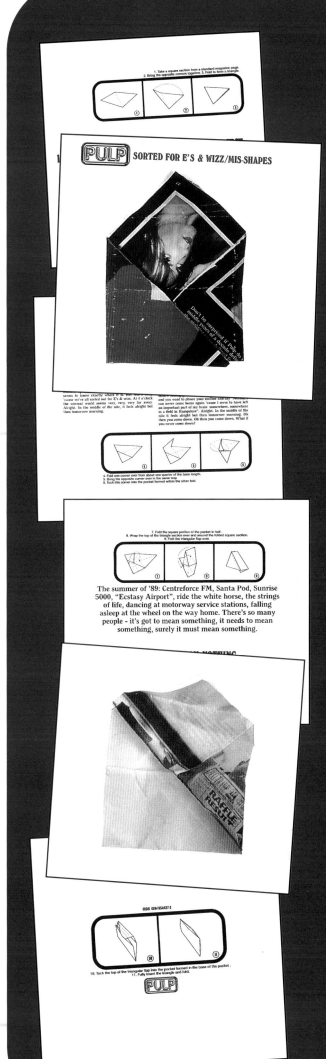

when it appeared hot on the tail of 'Common People'. Packaged in a sleeve which depicted a diagram for how to make a drugs wrap (the kind used for carrying speed and cocaine), the record provoked an outcry from The Daily Mirror's uptight Kate Thornton, who broke the story beneath a front page headline screaming **'Ban This Sick Stunt Now'.** A moral rant filled the inside pages, all of which did little besides showing the journalist to be ignorant of 'Sorted's so-what attitude towards drugs. Reluctantly Island changed the packaging, but it was a negligible triumph for The Daily Mirror, despite the fact that they gloated horribly afterwards.

The true irony of this situation was highlighted by Jarvis's written apology to the paper, in which he made tongue in cheek comments about preferring riding his bicycle to taking drugs.

In actual fact, the song had been written after Jarvis met a girl in a Sheffield nightclub who described the infamous Stone Roses gig at Spike

Island as being full of suspicious characters trawling about asking people if they were **"sorted for E's and whizz"**. The phrase simply stuck in his head, while the message was that drugs are really not such a big deal. Far from being a pro-drug anthem, if anything it was a reminder that life can offer much richer and more satisfying experiences than standing in a field somewhere in the Home Counties, wondering if you'll ever find your brain again.

"It got me on the front of the Daily Mirror I suppose," said Jarvis to *Ripple magazine*, **"It's the only way I'd ever get there. It was really silly, really a no news day. Daily Mirror boredom causes problems."**

"It's the hypocrisy that gets me, taking this high moral tone." he told *Melody Maker,* **"It's them who pointed out what the thing is for, and if they hadn't made such a big deal of it, people wouldn't have got so interested."**

'Mis-Shapes' was inspired by the gangs who roamed Sheffield while Jarvis was growing up, (and probably still do), the ones who wore white short-sleeved shirts, black trousers and loafers - the kind who'd call you a queer if you didn't look like them.

"The thing is, those people hunt in packs, whereas the misfits or mis-shapes, because of the fact that they're more individualistic, are easier targets." said Jarvis, explaining how the idea behind

LET THE BEAT GO ON

the song is that the misfits would form a gang of their own and take control. Having spent a large part of his life as an outcast, deliberately or not, as always Jarvis was speaking from experience.

Towards the close of 1995, Pulp released their second major label album to masses of generous praise. Titled *'Different Class'* and resplendent in interchangeable and interactive packaging (as seen on pages 62-63), the album scored top marks across the board, from the pop weeklies, the indie weeklies and monthlies and the national broadsheets alike.

A ccording to Russell Senior, Pulp had finally honed their sound to that of a real band with this record, rather than sounding like seven bands making five different albums. He believed there was more unity in the music, partly because the producer, Chris Thomas, played down the *'gimmick'* aspects of Pulp, and took them seriously.

Jarvis wrote all the lyrics for *'Different Class'* in just two nights. Fortified by cheap brandy he planted himself in his sister's kitchen and kept going until he collapsed. He commented that this time his songs were less obsessed with sad relationships and had more to do with situations he'd encountered since moving to London. They were more tied up with the shift from his East End squat survival days to the glamourous life of success.

"I prefer writing from my own experience as it's very difficult to get into somebody else's mind. I find it difficult enough to know what's going on in my own mind." he told *Outlook magazine*.

'Disco 2,000' was the final Pulp release for 1995. Lifted from the album , it related the tale of a boy's desire for the girl down the road. He's grown up with her, but never manages to win her over romantically. Inevitably she marries someone else, but years later he reappears in her life and tries to arrange a tryst with her. Typically realistic, it was no doubt based on some event in Jarvis's life, or that of someone he knows.

"Our songs are always based on real events." he explained to Adam Higginbotham of *Select*. **"They're always about normal things."**

And to prevent those normal things from landing in the kitchen sink, Jarvis employs the power of music.

"I think you should elevate mundane things into something quite epic, the music shouldn't be downbeat and pedestrian, it should be floating up there somewhere."

Explaining his philosophy of songwriting to journalist Nicola Barker, Jarvis said **"Once you've recorded a song it's dead because it can't develop anymore. It has to go out and live its own life. It's like a child that's reached it's 18th birthday and you say, "All right, it's been nice having you around, but go on, go out and earn your own living. Get out of my house."**

At least that way, there'll always be room for more. ●

REVENGE OF THE NERD

THE RISE AND RISE OF JARVIS BRANSON COCKER

"Anybody who is perceived to have some sort of success becomes attractive"

J arvis Cocker must be one of Britain's unlikeliest sex symbols. Unfeasibly tall and skinny, he cuts an incredibly peculiar figure with his long, spindly legs and pigeon chest. Yet he's managed to capture the imagination and sexual attention of thousands of adoring females, who probably want more than a chance to feed him up. He, of course, modestly puts his popularity down to his success. **"Anybody who is perceived to have got some sort of success becomes attractive,"** he said to the Telegraph magazine, **"Phil Collins gets girls, look at the state of him..."** Point taken. Success is a bit of a magnet. But nevertheless, Jarvis has a certain something which Phil Collins absolutely does not.

Speaking to Time Out's Laura Lee Davies, he admitted that because he bore no resemblance to Mel Gibson whatsoever, **"I do consider it as a triumph if someone considers me attractive."**

Physique doesn't really come into it. In the case of Jarvis Cocker, the attraction lies very much in the mind, in the fact that he's a people's hero, someone who's suffered all the self consciousness and social discomfort of being looked upon as something of an odd commodity, and has, above all, beaten it. And in that, there lies a very strong attraction, for the thinking and unthinking alike.

Jarvis Branson, like his name, was always extraordinary. Born to Christine, an art student, who gave up college for her son and ended up taking a job emptying fruit machines, and Mack, a struggling musician who deserted his family when Jarvis was only seven, the boy Cocker grew up with Saskia, his younger sister, and a whole bevy of female relations.

Mack and Christine met at the Sheffield University Rag Ball in 1962, where Mack played saxophone. A shotgun wedding was organised when Christine, previously a bit of a bohemian who hitch hiked round France and listened to Miles Davis records, got pregnant. Christine maintains that her estranged husband was a good father, but he was also a terrible liar, cheating her in financial matters. She admitted to the Mail On Sunday's Art McCulloch that she was actually relieved when he left.

Jarvis's first memory, as confessed to Sylvia Patterson in *Sky magazine*, is of being two and watching his mother suckle his new born sister. He asked if he could have a go, and when the reply was no, he couldn't figure out why Saskia could have something he couldn't. He doesn't however, remember much about his father leaving home, for which he feels guilty, but at least he didn't suffer like Saskia, who was quite badly affected when Mack departed to seek his fortune in London, having grown claustrophobic in his domestic set-up.

From Britain's capital, Cocker Senior travelled to Australia where he worked as a DJ and a rock journalist, as well as continuing with his music. He also battled with a drinking problem and an illness which encouraged him to spend some time in the desert.

"I know I take after my father because of things my family have said." Jarvis told the *Telegraph magazine*, **"Just the way I walk and talk, which is weird because I haven't seen him since I was seven."**

When he was about 17, and working as a fishmonger, Jarvis grew a little stripe of a beard right down the middle of his chin, just like Hugh Cornwell of The Stranglers. He kept it for a few years, but one day he saw a photograph of his father taken around the time his mother became pregnant, and it scared the hell out of him because he was going out with a girl who'd gone to the same art college as Christine. Thinking his life was going to follow the same twists and turns as his father, and that his girlfriend was going to end up pregnant, he shaved the beard off immediately, but still believes it was a peculiar coincidence that he grew it at all.

Managing without a father didn't seem to pose too many problems for Jarvis initially. But as he grew older the conflicts began to arise. His mother had to teach him to shave, which was quite amusing, as she obviously hadn't done it before. And until adolescence he'd assumed men and women were the same, so dealing with women on a sexual level was a little complicated. Being surrounded by women

had its benefits though. The female perspective so evident in many of Pulp's songs was probably a direct result of his environment. In addition to his immediate family, Jarvis lived in very close proximity to his grandmother, her sister, and his Auntie Mandy who lived across the yard and who had parties where people snogged on the stairs. A good deal of his mother's friends had been deserted by their husbands, including Auntie Mandy, and this destroyed Jarvis's faith in marriage. At the age of nine he heard some of them discussing how awful it was for a man to be nice, and failing to grasp such a confusing concept, remained irretrievably baffled.

Instead of dwelling too much on such complicated earthly matters, Jarvis chose to focus on higher things. He became consumed with the idea of living in space, and didn't even bother to learn how to ride a bicycle because he knew he wouldn't need one when he got there.

"I thought everyone would have established bases on Mars and things by about 1985," he said to Sian Pattenden in the *NME.* He even had a telescope, but it was a cheap one and he couldn't see the moon with it.

He also began to exhibit performance skills early on. At school during a game of Armies, he once played dead for 20 minutes with such alarming accuracy that an ambulance was called out.

In real life, Jarvis actually did have a brush with death. At the age of five he contracted a severe bout of meningitis, and all the children in his class from school wrote him letters and sent him presents. When he recovered, all of the gifts had to be destroyed because of the risk of infection, and Jarvis was left with seriously impaired eyesight. He returned to school wearing glasses, amidst peals of laughter.

Bespectacled, long-haired and clad in clothes stitched by his mother, the youthful Jarvis looked every bit the oddball. At Sheffield's City Comprehensive, he was bad at sports, unpopular with girls and worst of all bullied. Ignoring the latter solved that particular problem, but the others remained. Between the ages of 14 and 16 or 17 he became a recluse, retreating into his room after school where he'd tape music from John Peel's show on the radio and play his guitar, making music which his mother referred to as "plinky-plonk". He'd had a paper round, and was saving to buy Led Zeppelin's 'Physical Graffiti' because he liked the cover, and he used to go and look at it in Virgin Records, but hearing people like Elvis Costello on Peel's show changed his mind completely.

Worried about her son's hermit-like behaviour Christine secured him a job in an effort to boost his non-existent social life, but as it involved selling fish and scrubbing crabs, and therefore a lingering smell, it didn't have the desired effect.

Eventually Jarvis resigned himself to his eternal fate as an outsider, gave up all hope of trying to fit in, and instead threw himself into being utterly and gloriously inimitable. He began wearing high heels to exaggerate his height, he dreamt about being in a band while waiting in the dinner queue to make it seem more exciting, and finally he formed Pulp during an economics lesson, performing his first gig at school with special effects provided by some burning magnesium. His vocation in life had been found.

Being in a band did little to improve Jarvis's relations with the opposite sex though. He used to play Spin The Bottle in a cottage on the Derbyshire moors which his school owned, but he was never asked to do anything naughty. Once he got dared to walk into the girls' sleeping quarters through the loft, but not being aware of the need to balance on the rafters, he found himself crashing through the ceiling and ending up back where he started.

When he was 15 he had his first snog with a girl called Caroline, who became his official snogging partner. He knew her from school, but they never exchanged a word there, they just got together at parties and pretended to be married. Apparently she was boring and sported a particularly unattractive

REVENGE OF THE NERD

bowl haircut, and once she turned up at a party with a doll, informing Jarvis that she was filing for divorce and wanted custody of their child.

O n another occasion Jarvis found himself paired up with a girl renowned for "doing it" - in a bedroom. He left still holding onto his virginity, thanks to a severe lack of condoms, but had managed to acquire a huge lovebite as compensation.

In fact, Jarvis didn't actually have sex until he was nearly 20, by which time he'd already written numerous songs on the subject. Many of them were to appear on 'It', Pulp's debut album, which was just about to be released at the time he 'did it'. And after doing it, his romantic delusions were well and truly quashed, according to one of his versions.

"I wish no one had ever written songs and films about love and sex, because by the time I got round to doing it, it were right obvious that it wasn't the same thing. It was such an anticlimax. So I decided to be as down to earth and malicious as possible." he told Simon Price of *Melody Maker*.

In other interviews he has declared that his first time was refreshingly innocent as it involved himself and another virgin.

After he left school, Jarvis had the opportunity of a glowing academic career. He'd been offered a place at Oxford University, but flunked his interview when he pretended he'd read a book he hadn't. He was also offered the chance to study English at Liverpool University, but deferred it so many times that they eventually gave up asking, much to his mother's regret.

Instead of spending the next three years drinking, shagging and paying the occasional visit to the library, Jarvis developed an aversion to students and had a go at being a pop star.

"I was jaundiced towards students mainly because of things like Rag Week and Pyjama Jump where rugby player types would dress up in suspenders and negligees and go wild for one night."

To support himself as a confirmed non-student, he signed on, and worked his way through various jobs including a playgroup leader and a bingo caller at children's parties.

"When you're in a band you have an excuse to look at life differently," Jarvis told Simon Price of *Melody Maker*, **"You keep looking forward to this mythical day when life becomes exciting, thinking, 'I might be living in a one-room flat with a hole in the roof, no one likes me but give it another year and I'll be a pop star.'"**

out of character. She begged me not to do it, but I was in the mood. I'd say that was a turning point in my life. I began to get things together after that."

In an interview with Stuart Maconie for Select, Jarvis admitted that it would have been a pretty pathetic way to die - falling out of a window, and that the experience made him realise how random life is, that it doesn't have a golden thread running through it, and he decided to take stock of everything while convalescing - which he had to do a lot of.

A six week stay in hospital, followed by two months in a wheelchair (from which he continued to perform gigs with Pulp) encouraged Jarvis to think more about the present and less about the future, although it would take him another three years on the dole to actually make any real changes to his situation. But when he was 25 he finally decided it was time to do something more constructive than sit around and wait to be famous, so he moved to London and began a film course at St. Martin's School of Art.

During this time he became, by his own admission, a *"drug addict"*. Meaning he got into the rave scene and stuffed himself full of ecstasy presumably. It was the first trend he'd ever been interested in, and he surprised himself with his

Shortly after signing an ill fated deal with Fire records, Jarvis fell out of a window above the Sven bookshop in Sheffield's Division Street, and ended up shattered on the pavement below while passers-by gingerly stepped over him. The ensuing experience ultimately altered the course of his life. He'd been trying to impress a girl by walking around the outside ledge and ended up in a crumpled heap 30 feet below, with a broken pelvis, amongst other injuries.

"I'd seen someone do a similar trick the week before." he told *Just 17's* Sian Pattenden, **"When I did it it was just senseless bravado, which is quite**

enthusiasm for it. Still, as he put it to Maconie in Select, **"No way was I being a Goth. And I couldn't be a new romantic. I would have looked a tit in knickerbockers."**

Despite the distraction of the drug addled acid house phase, Jarvis never gave up on Pulp, and during his college course things perked up for his band considerably. His calling as a performer was finally fulfiled. Although his band mates will tell you it was never not being played out.

"He couldn't do anything else." said Russell Senior in an interview with *The Face*, **"You can sit down to watch Neighbours and he'll be pacing about the room, striking poses and putting on stupid voices,**

REVENGE OF THE NERD

speaking to the characters." Russell claims never to have seen Jarvis acting naturally. He should know.

In 1988, Jarvis shared a flat above a butcher's shop with Russell. He proceeded to fill up the entire space with funny little objects from jumble sales. Russell tried to stay in control by cramming it all into plastic bags, but it never worked. Apparently, Jarvis owned five full length mirrors. Needless to say, Russell never lived with Jarvis ever again.

A year later, Jarvis arrived outside Nick Banks' house with a Transit van full of his accumulated 'rubbish' all ready to move into the spare room. The minute Jarvis got there, he sailed off to a driving lesson, leaving Nick and his housemates to haul his stuff inside, and thereafter he plagued them by dotting gonks around the living room.

When Jarvis first moved to London, he lived in a squat, but was soon evicted and ended up moving into Steve Mackey's Camberwell apartment. Again, his clutter came with him, although Steve's fondest memories are of the singer disguising himself for his fortnightly trips to the dole office. At the time Pulp were picking up, so Jarvis would go to sign on wearing a battered old jumper and a grunge hat. The entertainment factor of living with Jarvis apparently compensated for his reluctance for domestic chores.

There are many Jarvis Cocker stories. There was the time he threw a tantrum on ZTV, a Scandinavian television show because the band's equipment broke down. He kicked the microphone across the stage, bashed his foot and narrowly missed Steve. He was once kissed by a topless 17 year old during a charity football match against Blur at London's Mile End. And there was the time when he was allegedly spotted having sex at a Menswear party. And let's not forget his debut as a Top Of The Pops presenter when he appeared on BBC1 flashing the inside of his jacket with *'I Hate Marti Pellow'* emblazoned all over it.

There are many, many more. Too many to tell here. Some of them can be heard in his lyrics, while others pour out during interviews, but all of them testify to the man's unique character, supporting the view that he is indeed, one of Britain's finest pop stars. He may have been a nerd once, but he certainly got his revenge on everyone who ever dared to laugh at his knobbly knees, myopic glare, thick rimmed specs or bizarre dress sense. These days he's a bona fide celebrity, admired and loved by all kinds of talented artists, from film directors like Mike Leigh, comedians like Jo Brand, fashion designers like Katherine Hamnett, and other equally distinctive and highly creative singers, like Bjork. (When Jarvis visited Iceland in 1995, Bjork lent him her housekeys so he wouldn't have to spend his holiday in an impersonal hotel.) He's made his mark, and quite spectacularly. Thank God he didn't go to University. ●

DISCOGRAPHY

SINGLES

MY LIGHTHOUSE / LOOKING FOR LIFE
Red Rhino RED 32 May 1983

EVERYBODY'S PROBLEM / THERE WAS
Red Rhino RED 37 September 1983

LITTLE GIRL (WITH BLUE EYES) / SIMULTANEOUS / BLUE GLOW / THE WILL TO POWER
Fire FIRE 5 December 1985

DOGS ARE EVERYWHERE / THE MARK OF THE DEVIL / 97 LOVERS / ABORIGINE / GOODNIGHT
Fire BLAZE 10 June 1985

THEY SUFFOCATE AT NIGHT / TUNNEL
Fire BLAZE 17 January 1987

MASTER OF THE UNIVERSE / MANON / SILENCE
Fire BLAZE 21 March 1987

MY LEGENDARY GIRLFRIENDS / IS THIS HOUSE? / THIS HOUSE IS CONDEMNED
Fire BLAZE 44 September 1990

COUNTDOWN / DEATH GOES TO THE DISCO / COUNTDOWN (Radio Edit)
Fire BLAZE 51 August 1991

O.U. (Gone Gone) / SPACE / O.U. (Gone Gone) (Radio Edit)
Gift GIF 1 June 1992

MY LEGENDARY GIRLFRIEND / SICKLY GRIN / BACK IN L.A.
Caff CAFF 17 August 1992

BABIES / STYLOROC (NITES OF SUBURBIA) / SHEFFIELD: SEX CITY
Gift GIF 3 October 1992

RAZZMATAZZ / INSIDE SUSAN
Gift GIF 6 February 1993

LIPGLOSS / DEEP FRIED IN KELVIN / YOU'RE A NIGHTMARE
Island IS 567 November 1993

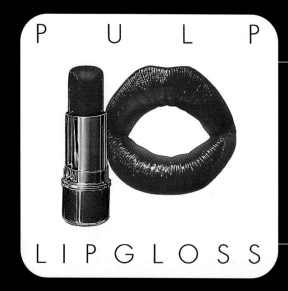

DO YOU REMEMBER THE FIRST TIME? / STREET LITES / THE BABYSITTER
Island IS 574 March 1994

THE SISTERS E.P. (Babies / Your Sister's Clothes / Seconds / His 'N' Hers)
Island IS 595 May 1994

COMMON PEOPLE / UNDERWEAR
Island I 613 May 1995

MIS-SHAPES / SORTED FOR E'S & WHIZZ
Island I 620 September 1995

DISCO 2000 / ANSAPHONE / LIVE BED SHOW
Island I 623 November 1995

IT (mini-LP)
Red Rhino REDLP 29 April 1983

FREAKS (LP)
Fire FIRE LP5 May 1987

SEPARATIONS (LP & CD)
Fire FIRE 11026 July 1992

FREAKS (CD)
Fire FIRE CD5 April 1993

PULPINTRO - THE GIFT RECORDINGS (LP &CD)
Island IM 2076 October 1993

HIS 'N' HERS (LP & CD)
Island IS 8025 April 1994

MASTERS OF THE UNIVERSE
- PULP ON FIRE 1985-86
Fire FIRE 36 JUNE 1994

DIFFERENT CLASS
Island I 8041 November 1995

LET'S MEET UP IN THE YEAR 2000

And they all lived happily ever after? It's a nice thought, but this isn't a fairy story. The frog may have turned into a prince, but no one kissed him to make it happen. He made it all happen with sheer graft and limpet-like tenacity. And he certainly isn't foolish enough to believe in it lasting forever. If anything he's worried about the luxury of stardom blurring his vision of cold, grey fumblings on plastic car seats amidst chip wrappers and empty beer cans. When you're travelling in limousines life certainly isn't normal. Still it's all fuel for thought, and Jarvis Cocker is a man who doesn't miss a beat. He may have